Fifty
Shapes
of Grey

Fifty
Shapes
of Grey

P J Thales

PENDULOUS PRESS

For information contact Pendulous Press, www.pendulouspress.com.

This is a work of satirical fiction. Names, characters, businesses, places, events and incidents are either the products of the author's imagination or used in a fictitious manner. Any resemblance to actual persons or things, living or dead, or actual events is purely coincidental.

ISBN: 978-0692459485

Pendulous Press
www.pendulouspress.com

First Edition

10   9   8   7   6   5   4   3   2   1

The Square. Four sides. Four corners. All equal—in angle, in length, in grandeur. This is a shape that looks you in the eye and says, 'I'm a solid geometric construction. Turgid even.' Mmmm... mama like. The square will see you now.

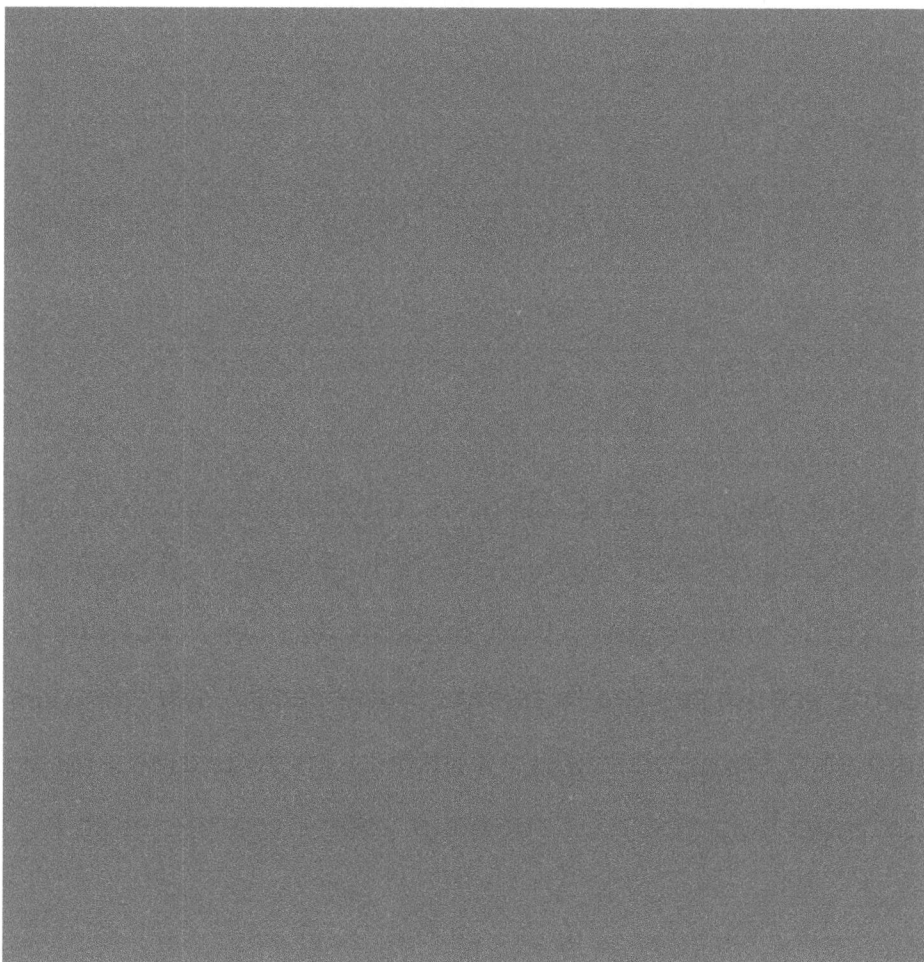

Square

Does it have no sides? Or does it just have one side that keeps going All. Day. Long. And all night. And all day again. The Circle never stops going, whether you want it to or not. Some people say that's pushy. Some people say it makes them sore. Some people say a little pi on your diameter will always help you find out what your circumference is.

Circle

This one is pointy.

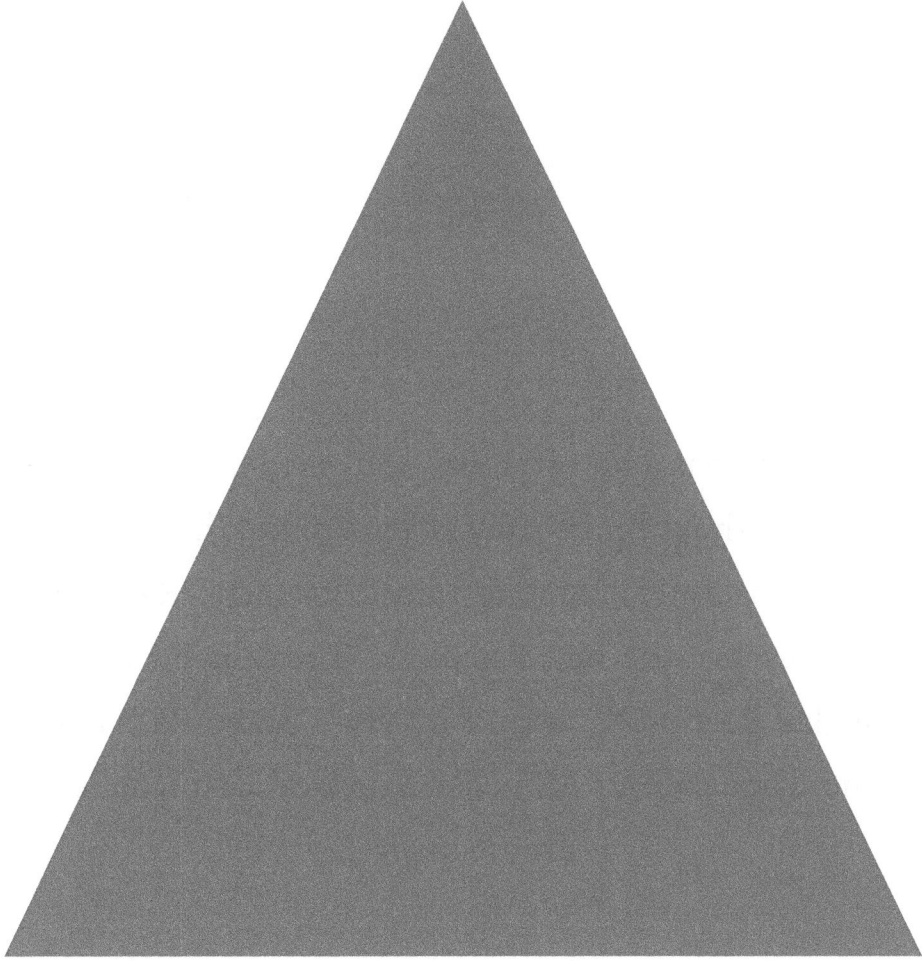

Triangle

The Rectangle is a bit of a diva—it likes to think of itself as a square without limits. Stay sharp around this character, as he's constantly changing names: Rectastic, Rectacular, Rec Specs, Rec-the-Mic, Rectangle "The Killa Fo' Cornas" Douglas, Rectum X., Sean "P-Diddy" Combs, ReX-Tina... This shape collects AKAs like a dodecahedron collects obtuse angles.

Rectaculous

They say diamonds are a girl's best friend--but who are THEY in the first place? The corporate romance-industrial complex? The vapid modern cult of consumerism? The heartless, exploitative heirarchical systems of our so-called society?!? No one knows...

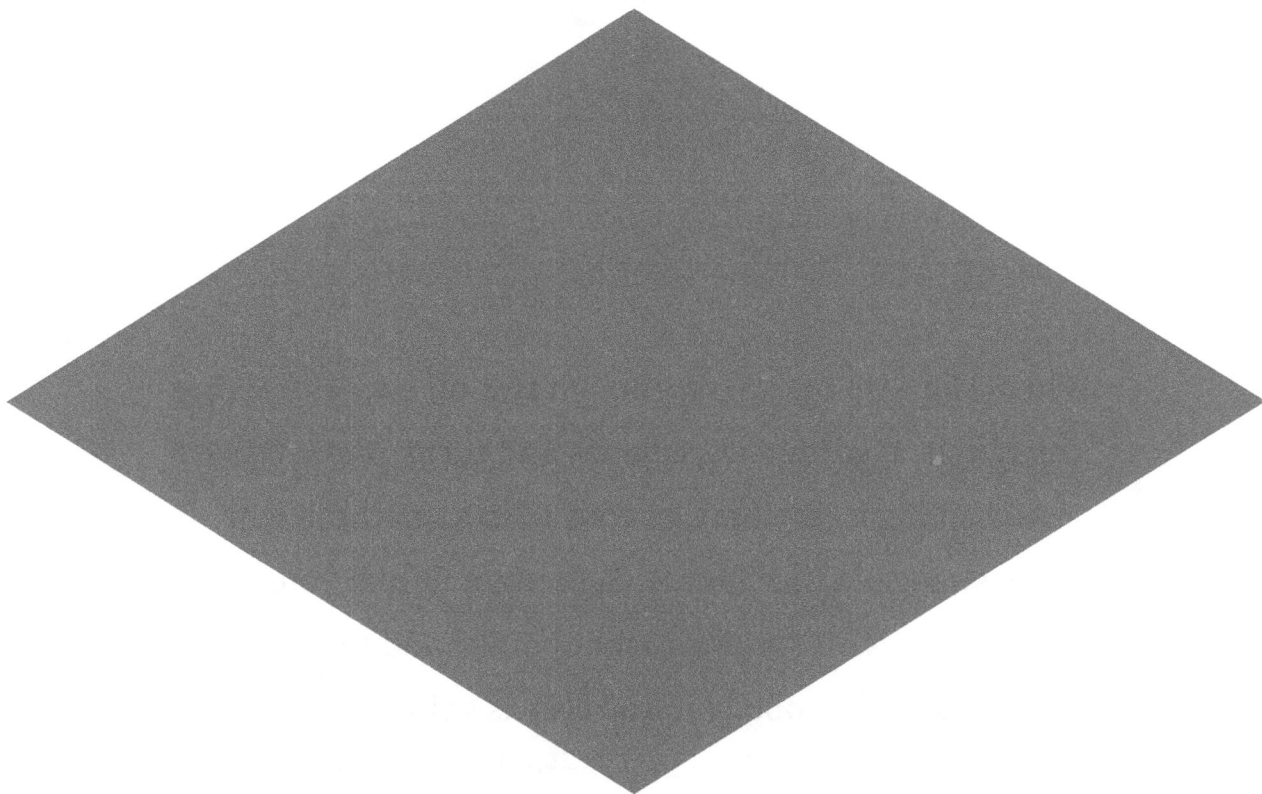

Diamond

When a Square has taken enough shit off a trash-talking rectangle, it gathers its cojones and turns into a Cube. And changes its name, of course, to something with some swagger... like Samuel L. Batman. When you come sauntering in with six sides, eight points, and twelve sharp-ass lines on you, nobody in the club is going to even think about pulling any funny business.

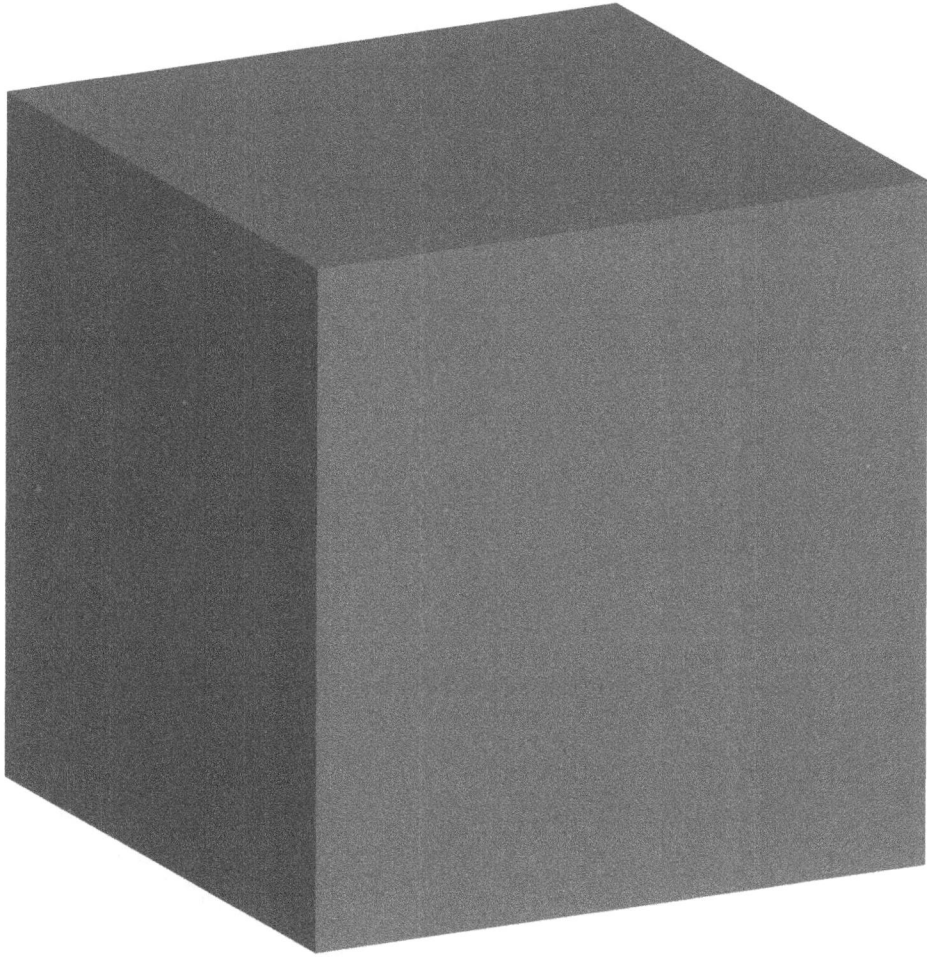

Samuel L. Batman

Eight sides, eight vaginas. That's how the Octagon keeps it tight while pumping out little octos, quads, and quints (yeah, different partners, dude—step off with your Puritan bullshit, it's the 21st century!). This shape knows what it wants, and right now, reader, it wants YOU.

(turn page quickly to avoid
intercourse with eight sided polygon)

Octamom

Yeah. It's a weird circle.

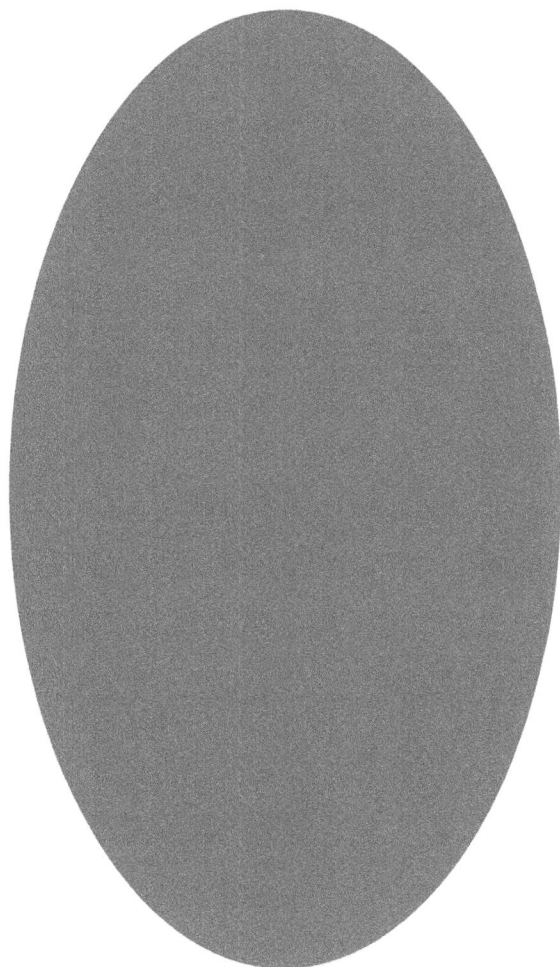

Oval

The Parallelogram, known in his home country as Slajovk Nmnenski, came to America in search of prosperity, love, and a cure for his aching back. All he found, alas, was a land of dick pics and beer helmets.

Fortunately, he likes that, too.

Slajovk Nmnenski

The humble Trapezoid may be quiet on the outside, but she's open to anything. Look at her one way, she's got all her ducks in a row. Look at her the other way, she's stolen all your ducks and is making them watch while she acts as a sturdy and inexpensive foundation block for a new deck or small DIY home addition.

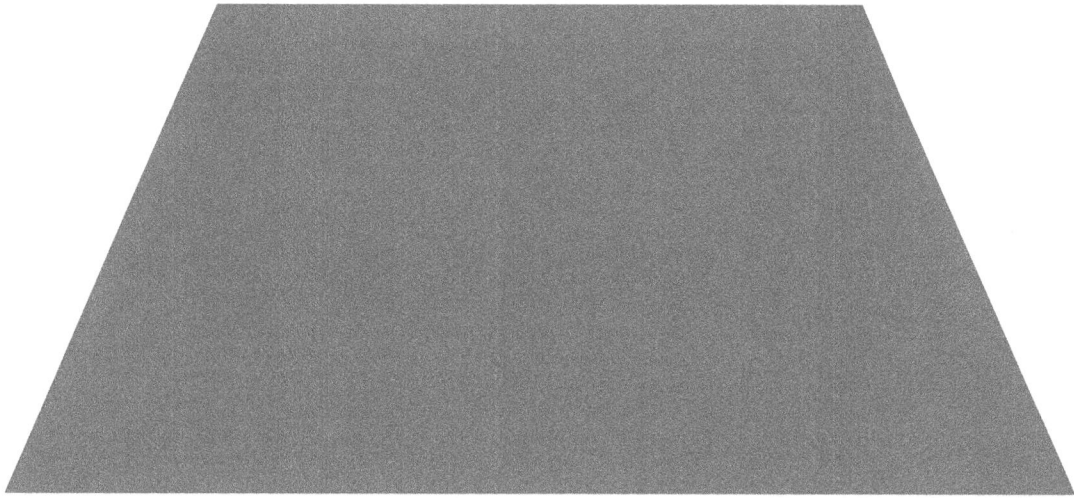

Trapezoid

What the Trapezium lacks in subtlety, she makes up for with sheer sexual abandon. Look at that one-shouldered shrug, just inviting a lucky someone to explore the true meaning of asymmetrical bliss.

Trapezium

"The boy's just too danged round!"

Those were the words this Sphere's circular father exclaimed when Too-Round Steve was born. As it turned out, his mama had been experimenting with some sticky-icky substances that gave her genes a serious penchant for the third dimension. Don't feel bad for the guy, though, he tends to let things like that roll right off him.

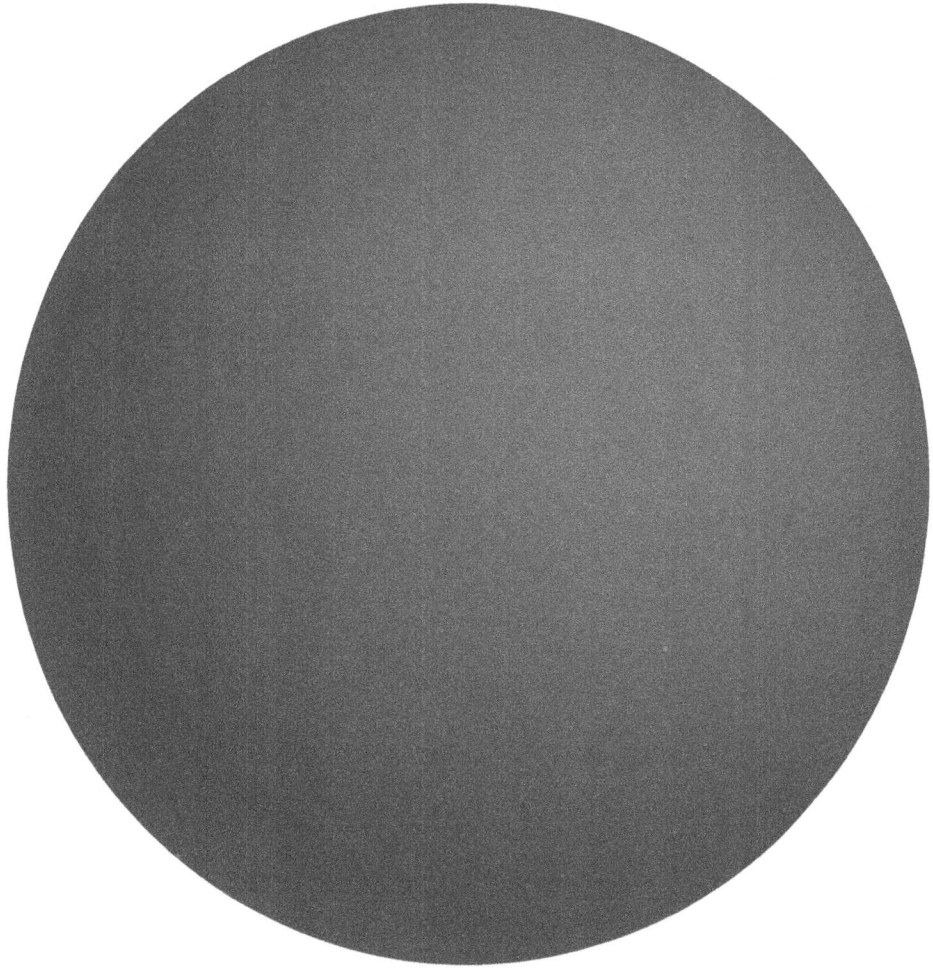

Too-Round Steve

Is he a fat stick or a tall disc? A wide wheel or a short pipe? The Cylinder tends to defy categorization, but he never defies your demands. Hollow or solid, soft or hard... he's whatever you need him to be, baby.

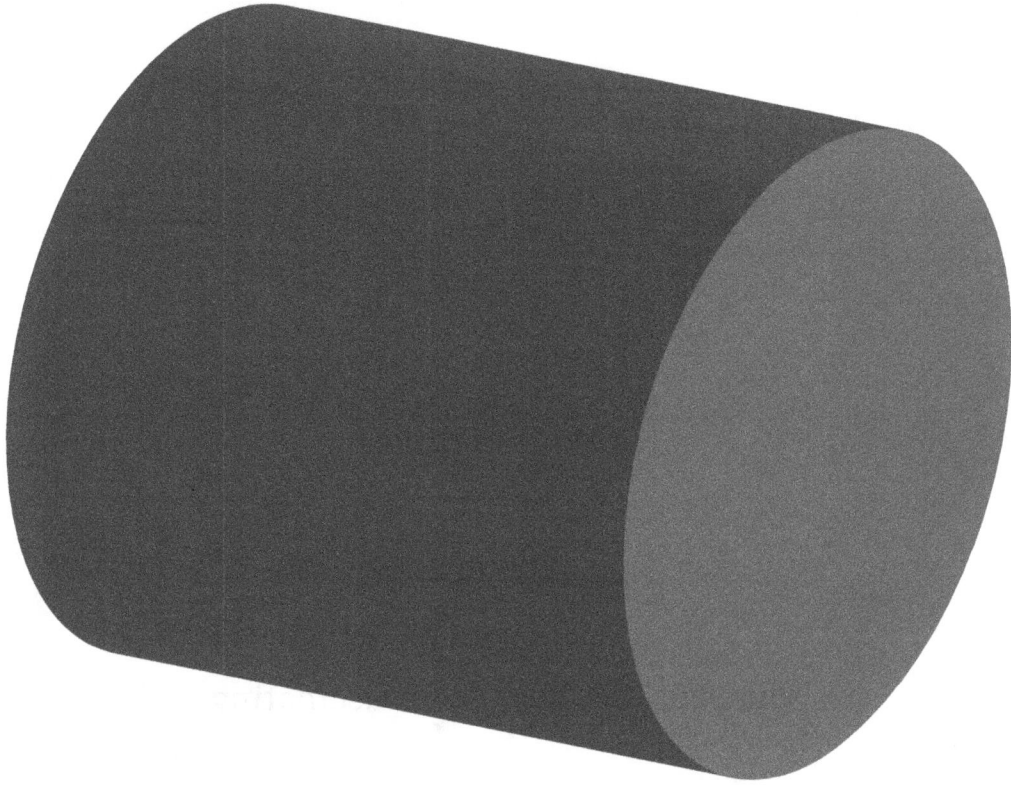

Cylinder

LOOK! UP THERE!

That's her mantra.

Whatever it is, it must be fascinating.

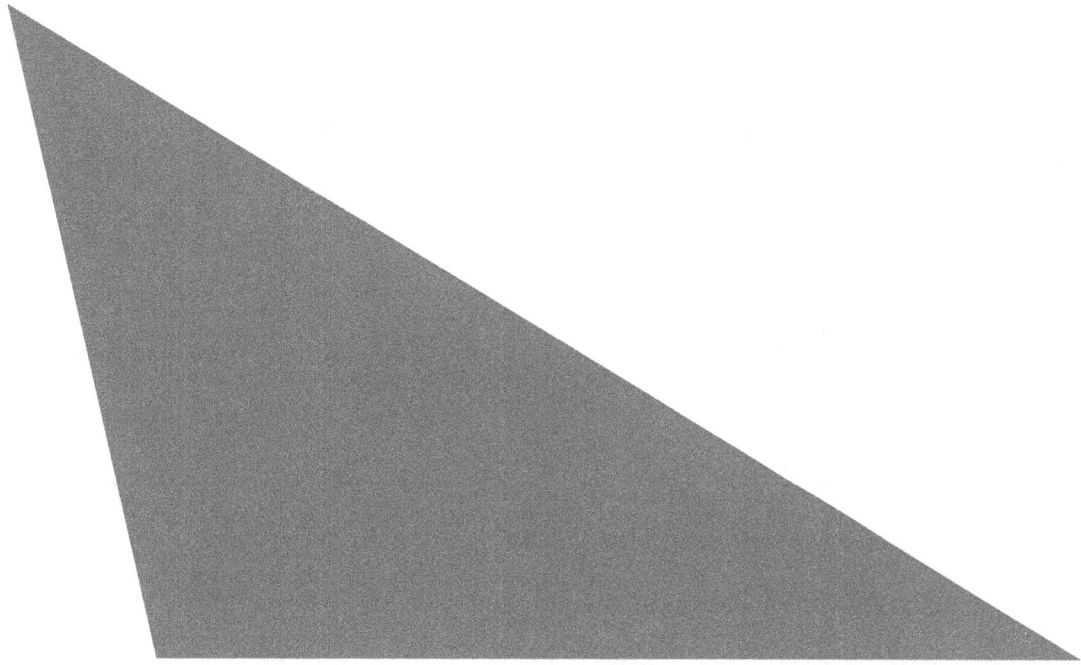

Obtuse-angled Scalene Triangle

She's a great improviser.

She knows what she wants, and what she wants is MORE.

More life, more love, more lust. Because she's paid her dues and has the battle scars to prove it. If you get involved with this Plus Sign, be prepared to strap in, because she leaves nothing behind, and when one train leaves San Antonio travelling at 65 miles per hour and a second train blah blah blah, you know she'll be somewhere up in that mix.

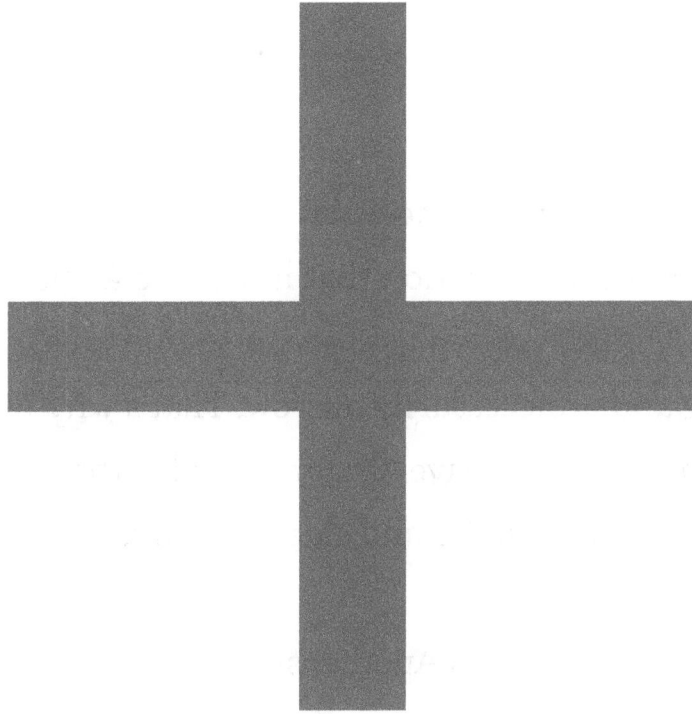

Plus Sign

You know that guy you meet at a party and you mention in the course of conversation that he's a Rectangle and he's all like, "Actually, I don't subscribe to that label. I find it limiting and unnecessarily narrow. That's why I identify using the more inclusive 'Quadrilateral.' What are we all but angles and sides anyway?"

That's Apotheosis Jones.

(And, yeah, that's not his real name,
as though you needed to be told.)

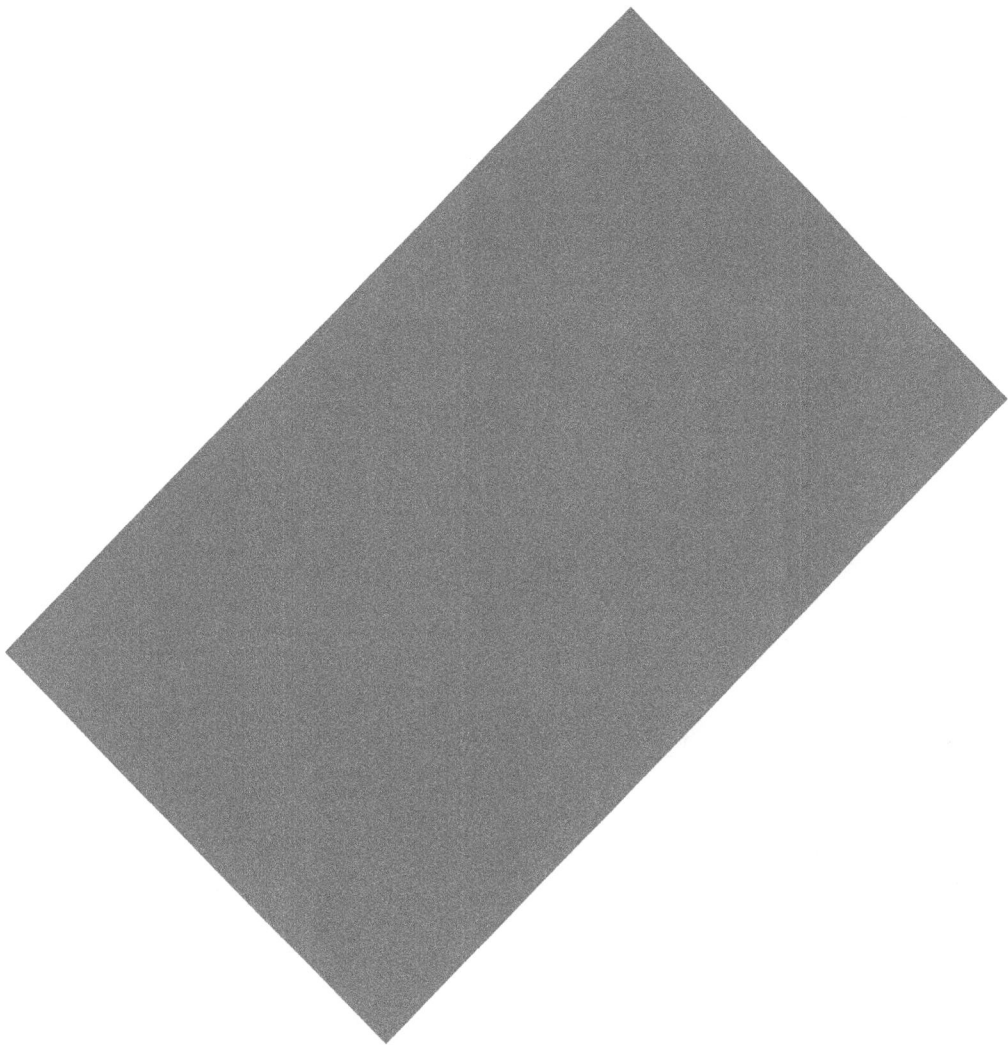

Apotheosis Jones

Two more sides.

You know what that means...

Two more angles.

Decamom

"If you're going to point, do it with some fucking class!"

This is a common refrain when the Chevron's had a couple tequila sunrises. You'll find him on the arms of soldiers, in the details of a tapestry or your grandfather's blazer, or snazzing up bitchin' coats-of-arms. Where you won't find him is rocking your world in the sack. Because, as you can see, the Chevron has no penis.

Chevron

The mystic lovechild of a Triangle and a Cone, the Pyramid keeps it pointy, and while she certainly doesn't mind a hysterical romp with a stranger, don't get any ideas that she's some kind of crazy. That low center of gravity keeps this lady stable as Clark Gable.

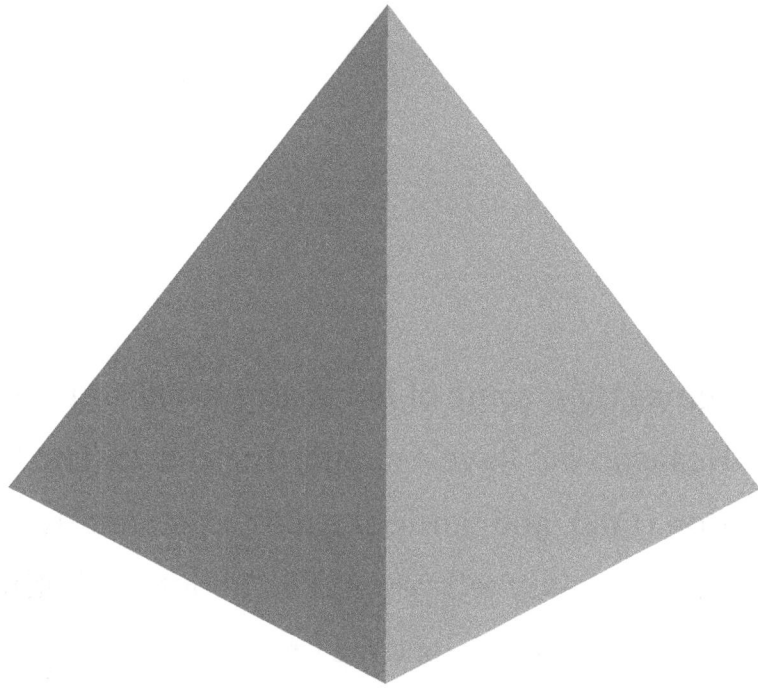

Pyramid

Fewer vaginas than some of her many-sided counterparts, but the Hexagon did have a supporting role in The French Connection (1972), and while she didn't personally win an Oscar, she'll certainly tell you ALLLL about it whether you have the time or not.

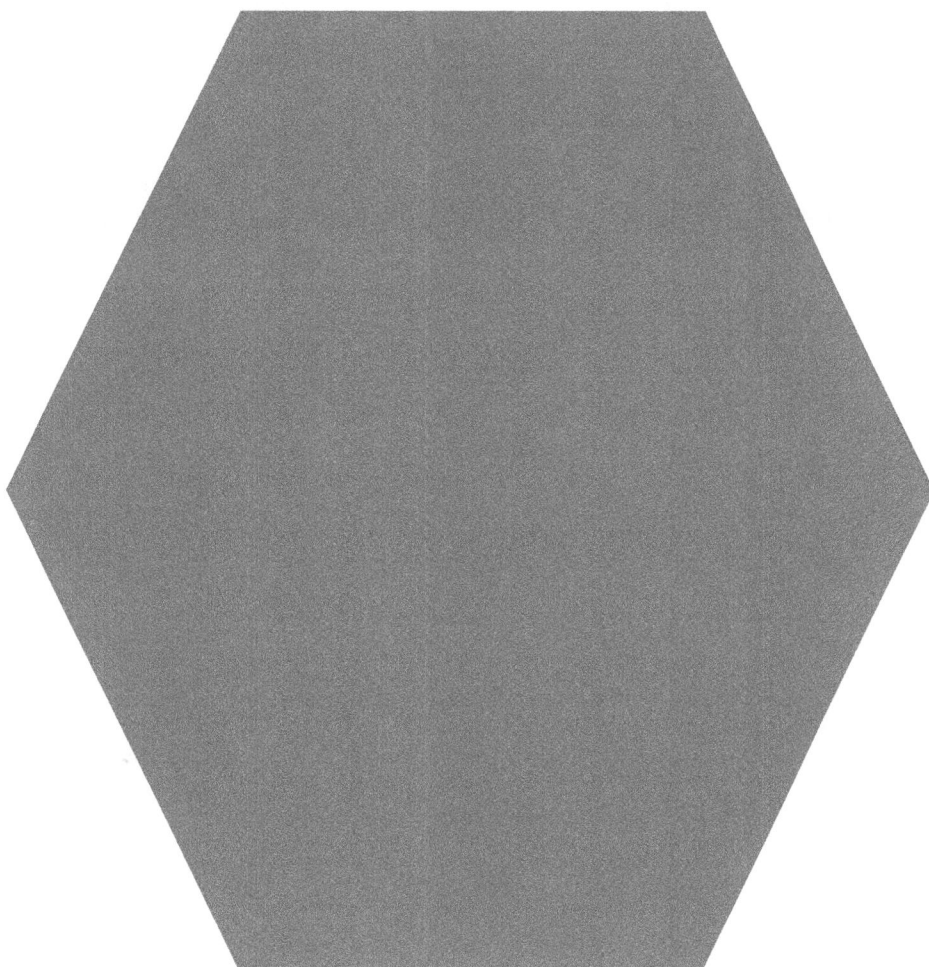

Hexagon

"When she feels your touch as she wakes in the morning,
When she sees the dishes you stayed up late to clean,
When she hears your song on the radio at lunchtime,
When she tastes the dinner you brought home at night,
When she hears from the hallway those tiny feet that you
created together,

She has the *sense* to know... it's love."

Jesus, Carol. Do these cards come with a barf bag?
Get a real job.

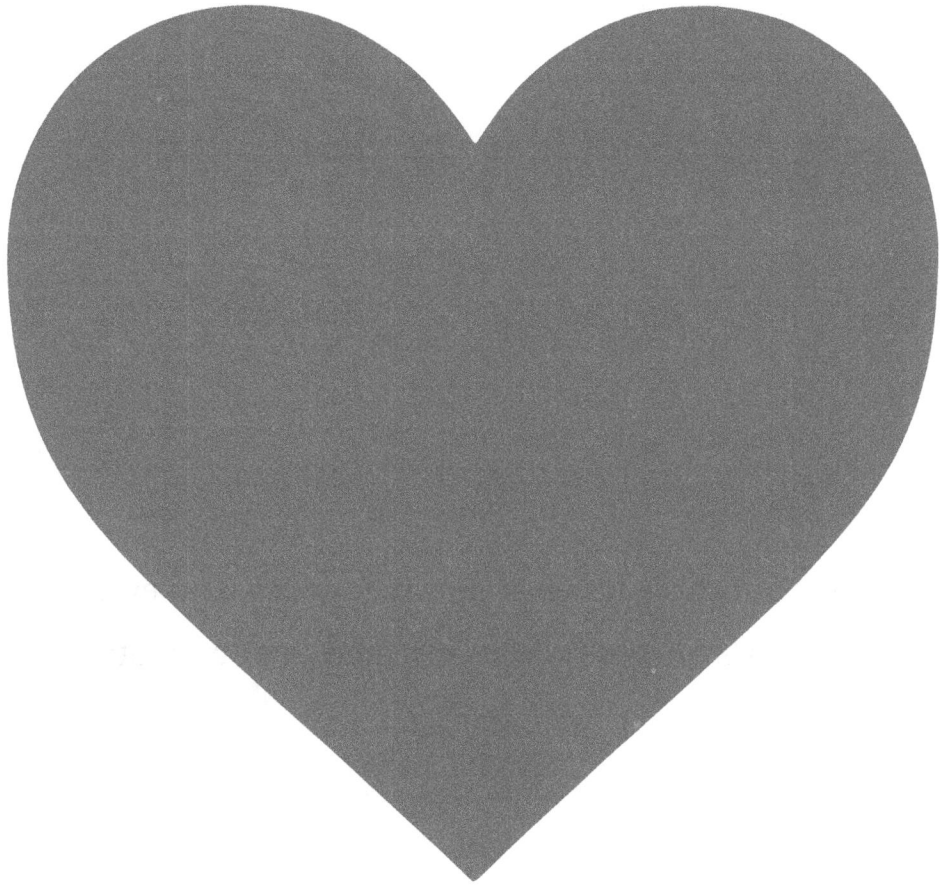

Carol Cares-a-lot

He snuck out three times at summer camp, and ever since then, he's known he was destined... to be... a Star!

C.J. Meeders

Suck it, Meeders.

Six-pointed Star

Isn't this starting to get a little ridiculous, guys? Maybe Apotheosis Jones is right. Can't we all just get along?

Rectangular Prism

Those who can, point. Those who can't... point less. No one does it better than the Sun, who's a bit of a prickly lover but worth it if you learn how to give her what she likes. Don't count on her if what you're looking for is a long, loving relationship, though. She tends to burn out after about 9.6 billion years.

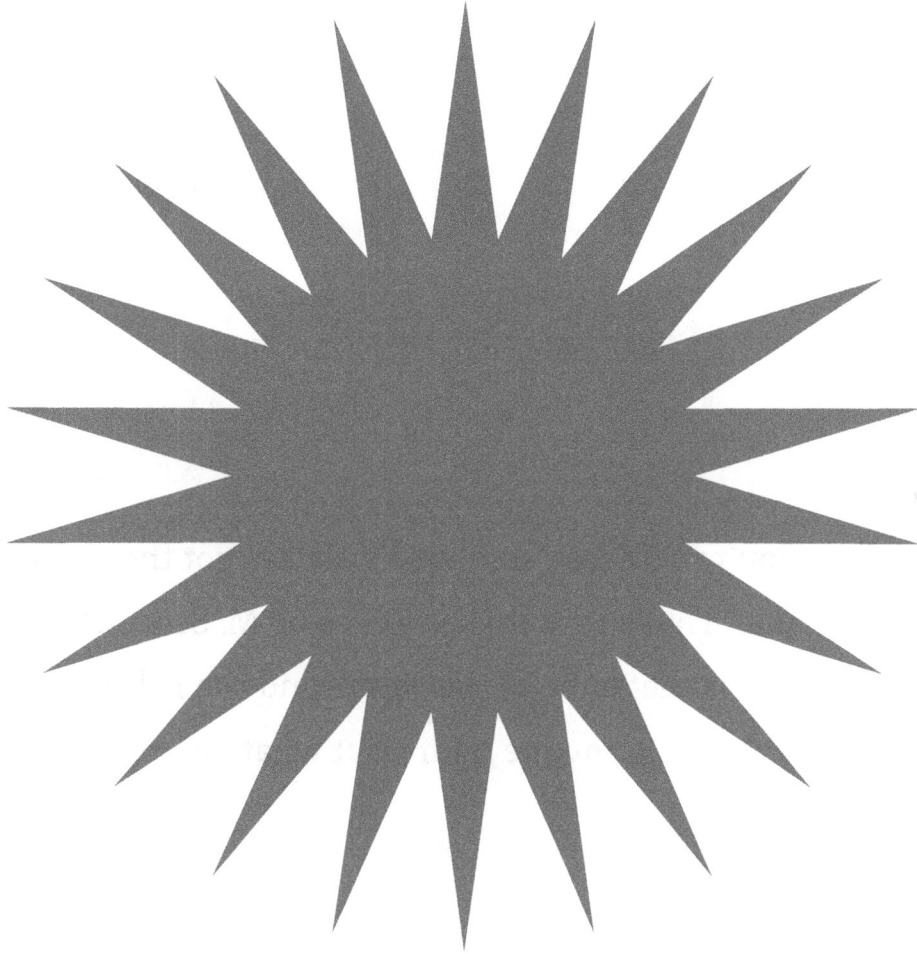

Sun (Twenty-two
Pointed Star)

When you're a Target, someone's always got their aim set on you. That's why this one goes by M. Scott Davis. Anonymity is the name of the game, and the rules of the game are don't let anyone figure out what you really are.

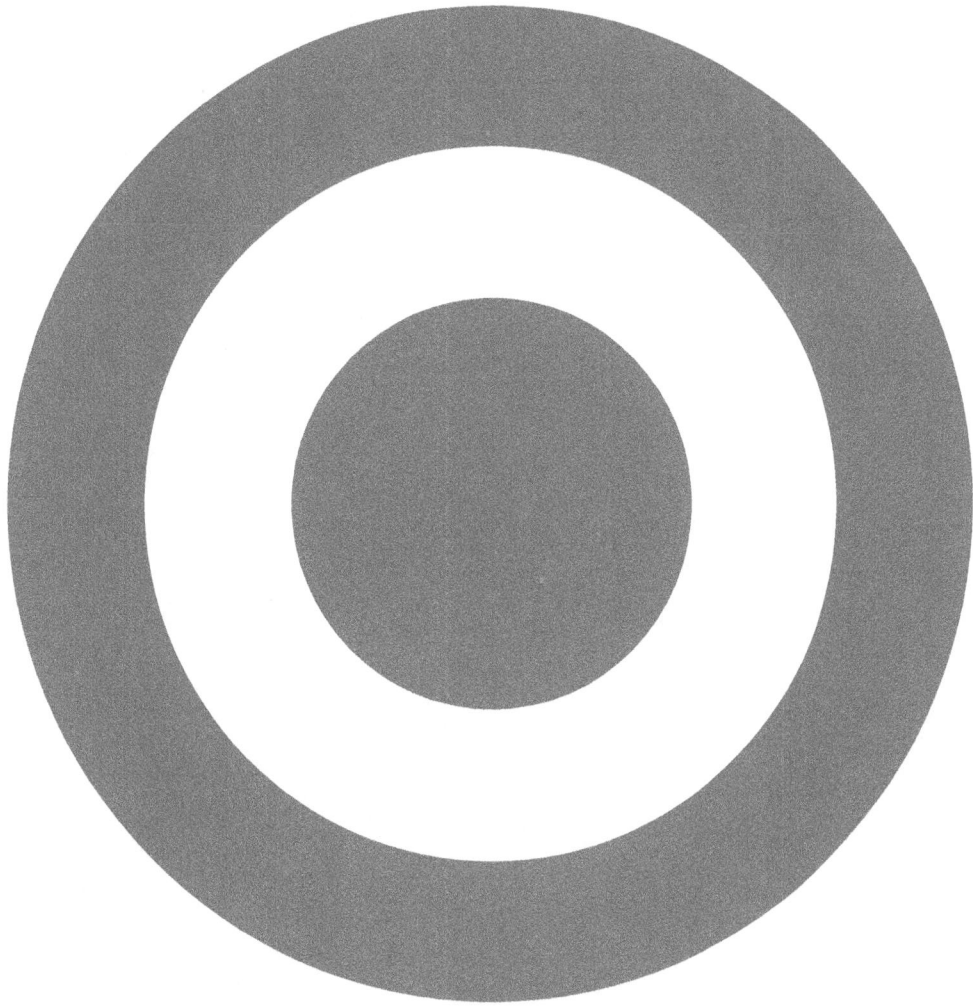

M. Scott Davis

NO! NO! IT'S REALLY OVER THEEEEEEERE!

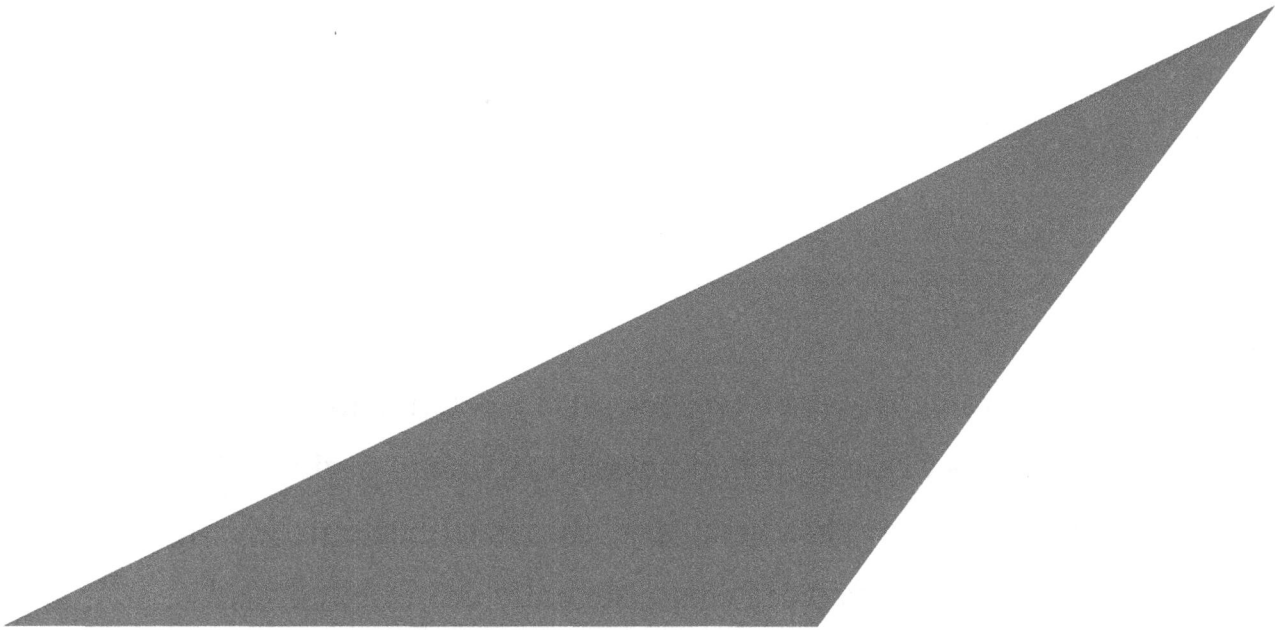

Obtuse-angled
Isosceles Triangle

The Crescent was a Crescent until it wasn't, and once it wasn't a Crescent it had never been one to begin with. There is, always has been, and always will be only Mystic Mike, and if you are clean, sexually uninhibited, and have $49.99, you can join the Sacred Temple of Bread and Wisdom and find out how Brother Mike came into the light and found his being.

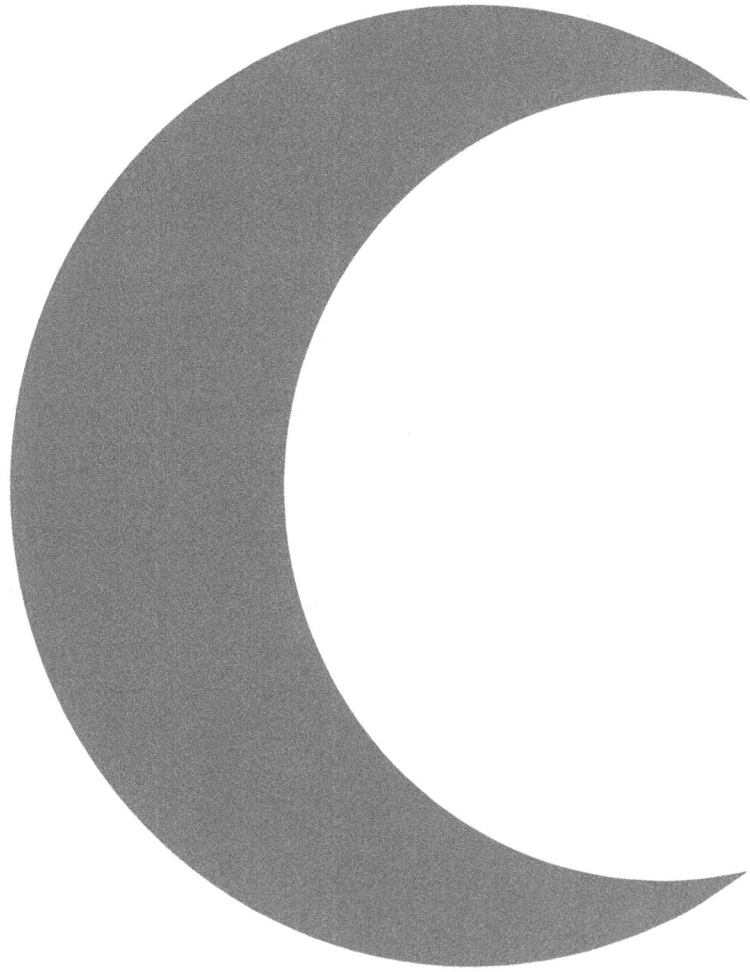

Mystic
Mike

"Pass the teabiscuits, won't you, love? And don't forget the jam and cheese but make sure to hand it gracefully. And— heavens me!—tuck your shirt in while in the presence of guests! Were you raised in a barn? We keep our clothes wrapped firmly round our bodies in this household... until we don't of course. Once the Helmsleys take their leave and the help has all retired to the basement I'll bite you in two like the salty little peanut you are. Grrrrrrrrrrrrrrrrrrrrrrrrrrrrrrrr..."

(turn page quickly to avoid BDSM experience with classic design element... remain on page to enjoy)

Quatrefoil

What's there to say? It's one of the classic geometric
patterns identified by Pythagoras.

And it's damn sexy.

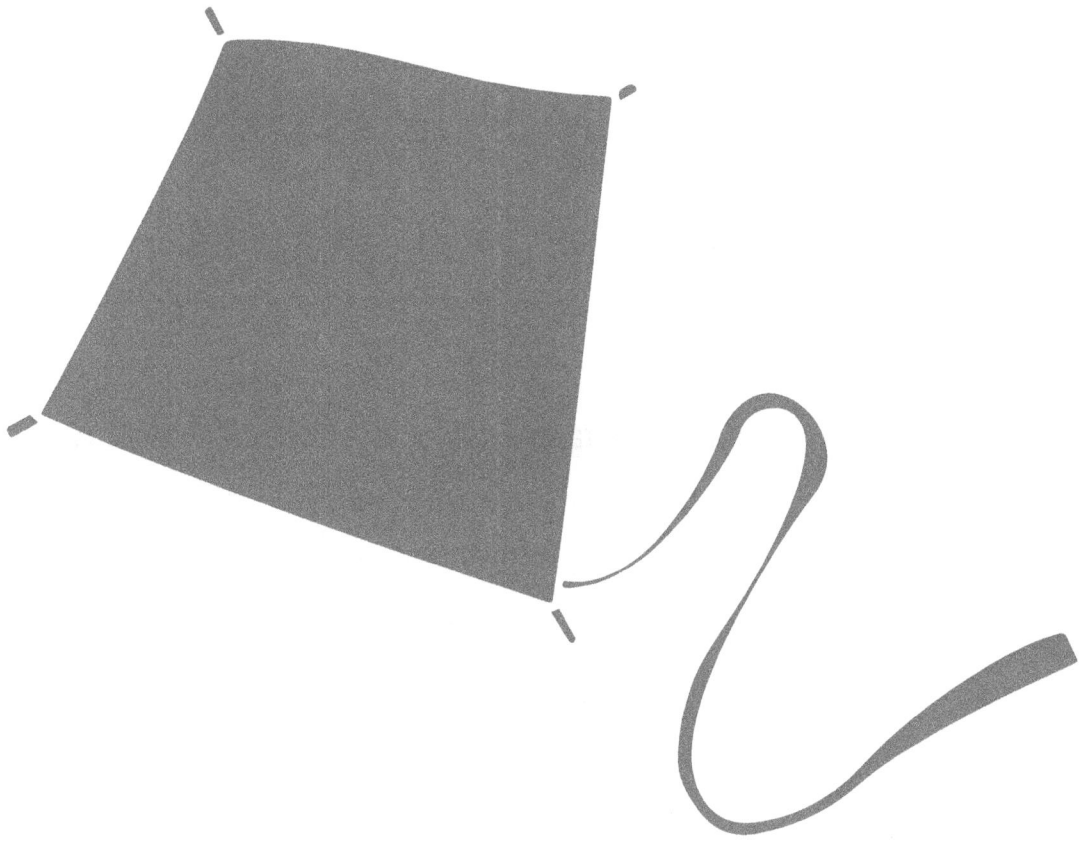

Kite

He's so soft he's so cuddly he's so squishy and lovey and nuzzly and pretty and sweet I love him I love you Mister Biggles and your little ears and your little tail and your little nose and your little face let's be friends for ever and ever and ever and ever and ever and ever and ever and look how he hops with his cute little feet and wiggles his nose we should call him Mister Wiggles instead of Mister Biggles shouldn't we Wister Sniggles...

Someone clean the shit out of this cage.

Mister Biggles

He's a fifth semester sophomore and he's majoring in boobs and hashish.

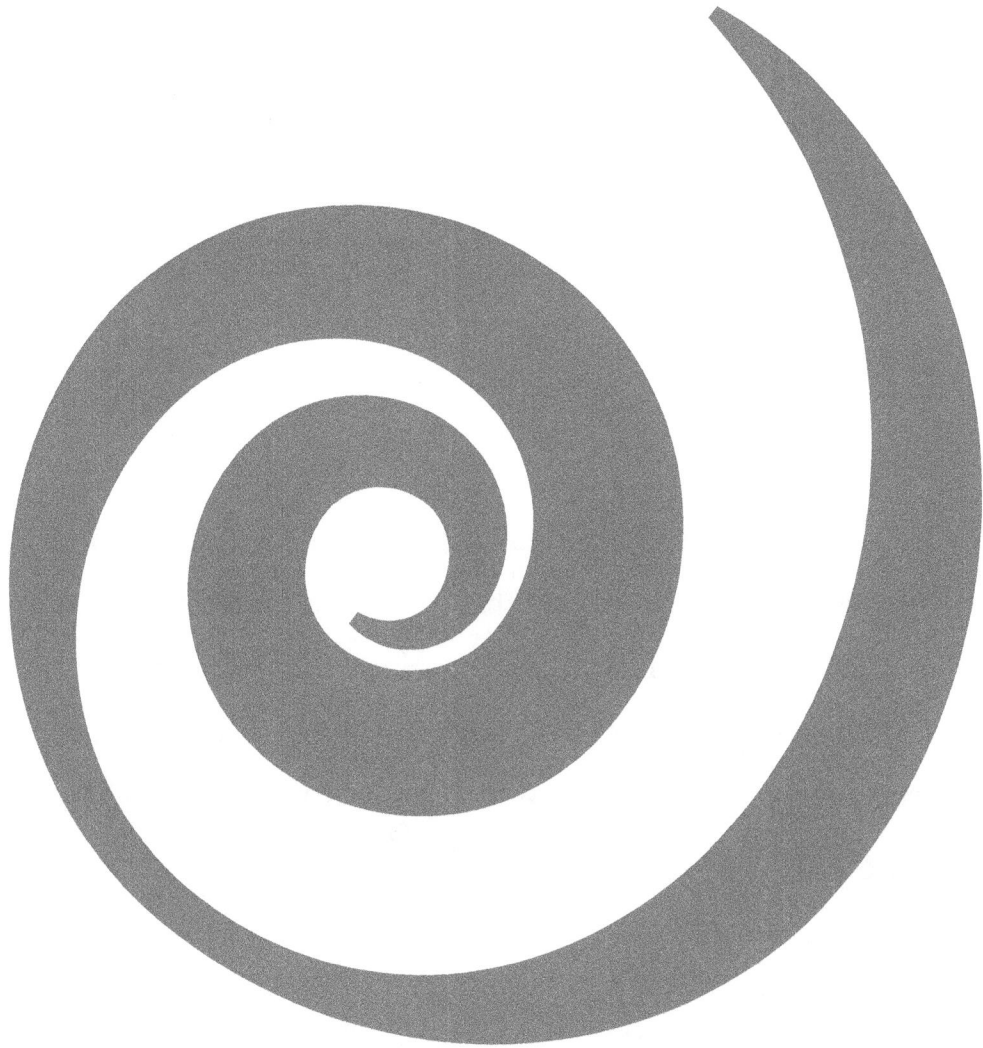

Carlos
Fantasmo

No one knows exactly what it is, you know? It's hard to put your finger on it, but there's just something about her that—when you try to categorize or come up with the words to explain you just, sort of—I wish I had a more precise word to describe her but all I can really say is that she's just... a bit... odd.

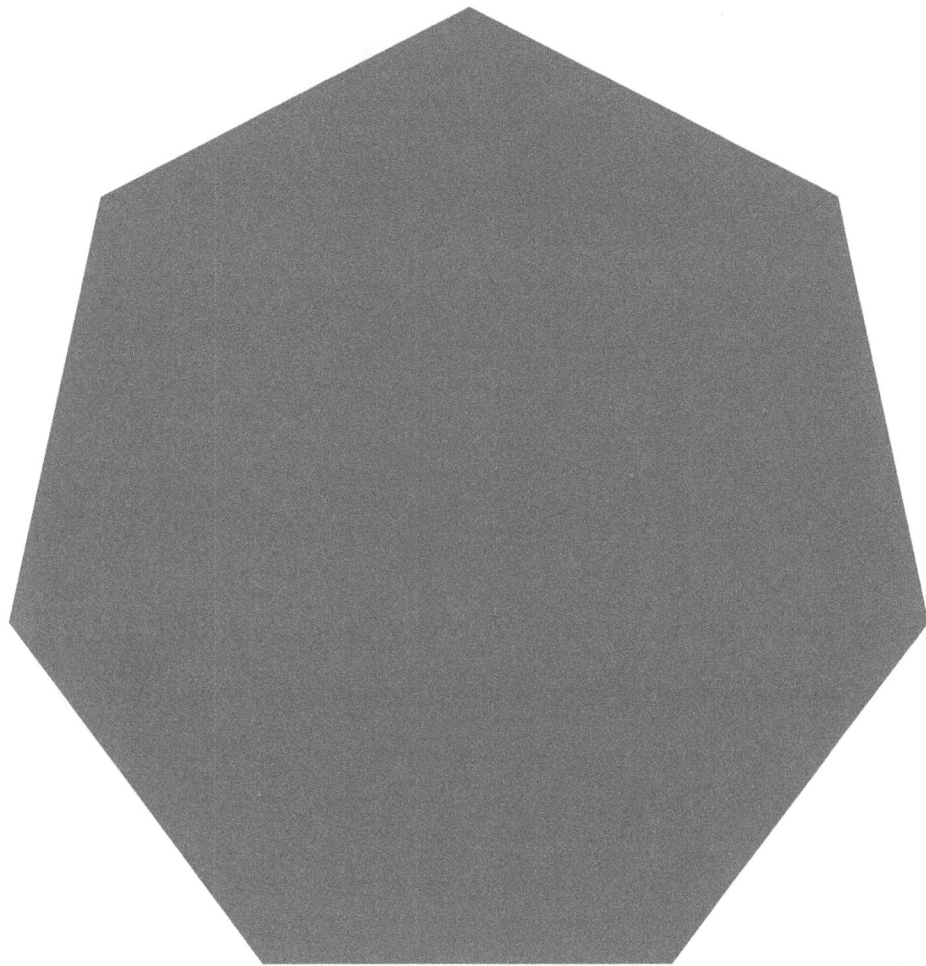

Hepzibah
O'Flanaghan

Okay, Betty, we trust you. You're the one who REALLY knows where that thing is that everyone's looking for.

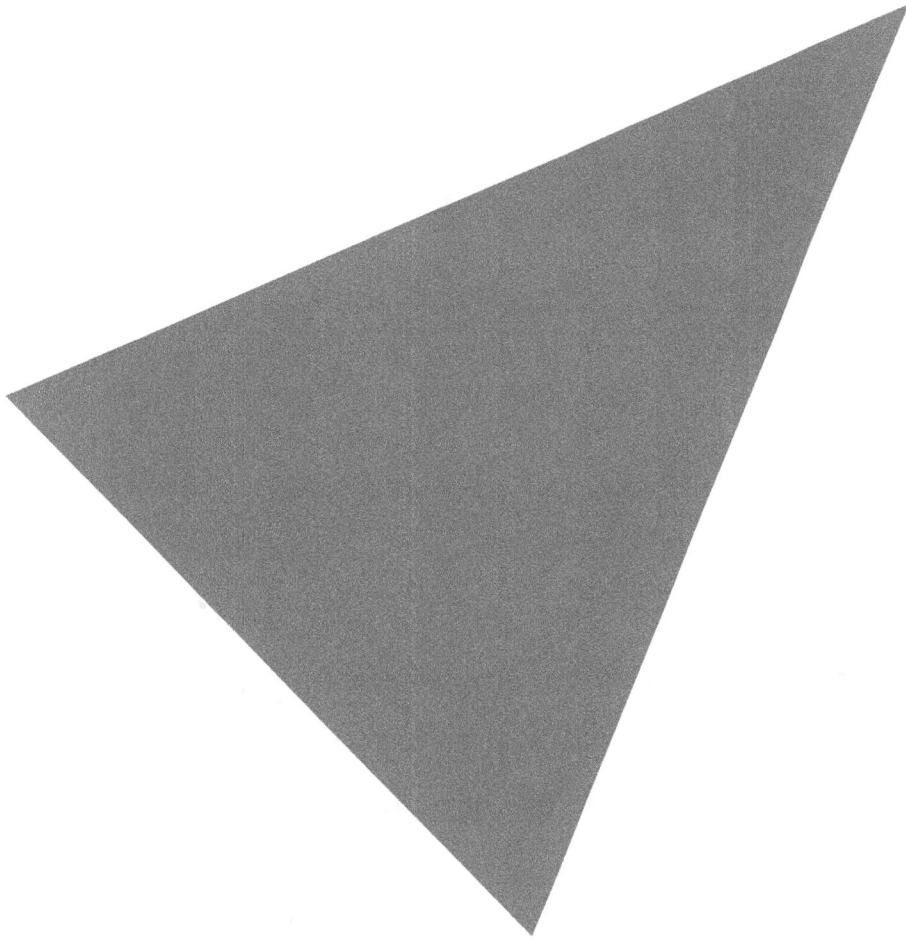

Betty Rexler

Aaaawwww yeeeeessssss. He's smooth... and he's round... and he keeps on going and going for as long as you like. That's cool Lev, the Torus with the More-us. And he don't discriminate, baby, so bring ya damn self down to Lev's beachside bungalow and see if you can make his large hadron collider start spinnin'.

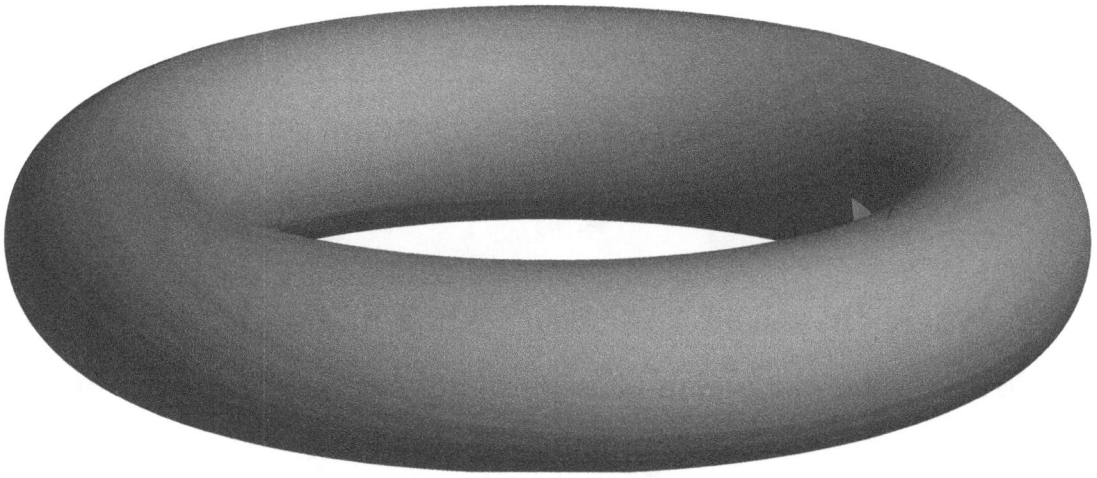

Lev Urbanks

You are looking at Rosalind, and you are getting very,
v e r y   s l e e p y.

Where did you go, Rosie Bear? Who's in the what how?
Where's the place? Am I the swinging monkey? Are you the
swinging hapsflapper?

Say the word. Say some words. Say the word say. I don't
know when the flerbutter misangulates for President
Snippideedip. Ros? Rooooooooooooooozzzzzz.

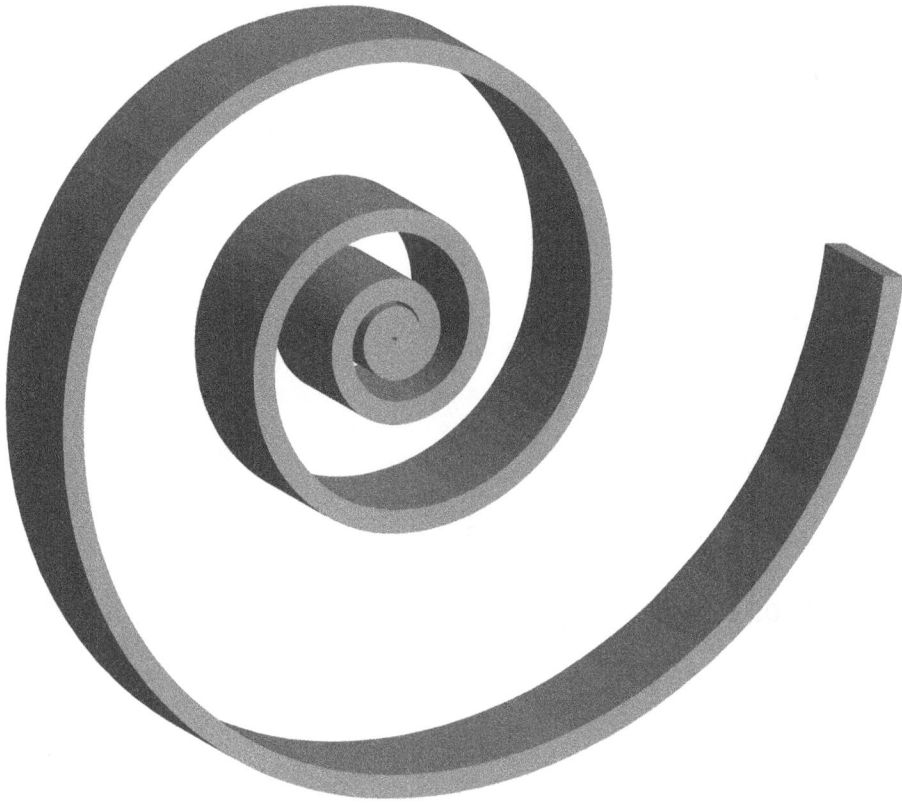

Rosalind Franklin

Right angles? More like Right Angels. Krassi is classy and she keeps it tight, ninety degrees, all day and ALL night.

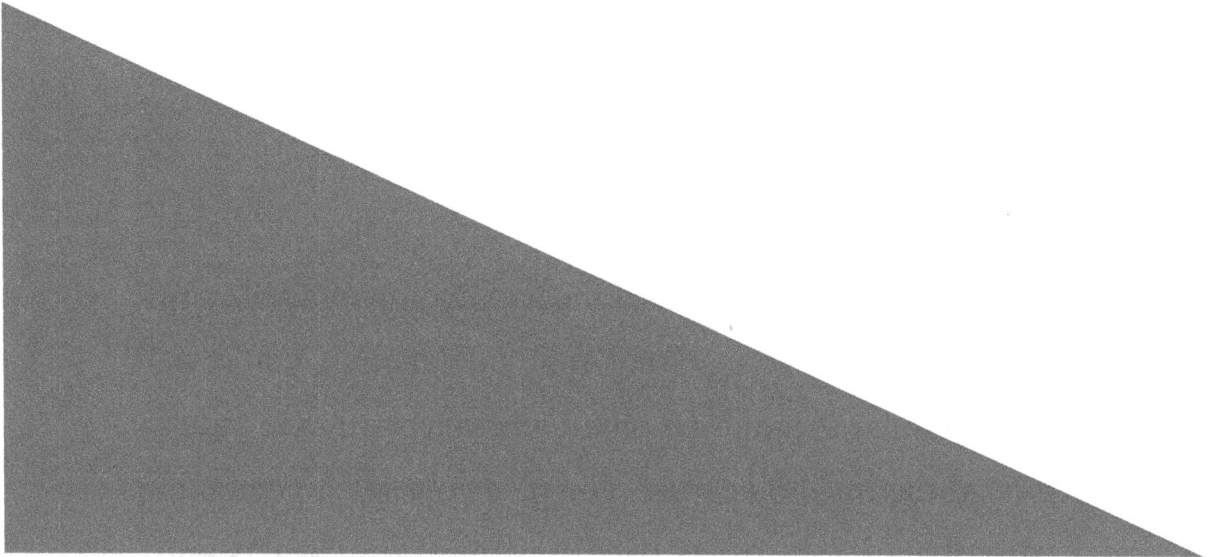

Krassi
Stephanopoulous

Pretty much the final word in the ongoing quadrilateral scuffle. When you go long and you got girth, you're a Rectangular Prism. And when you've got all that plus a flourishing hip-hop career, you give yourself a new name. And if your day-to-day consists of breaking hearts and breaking homes, that name might as well be...

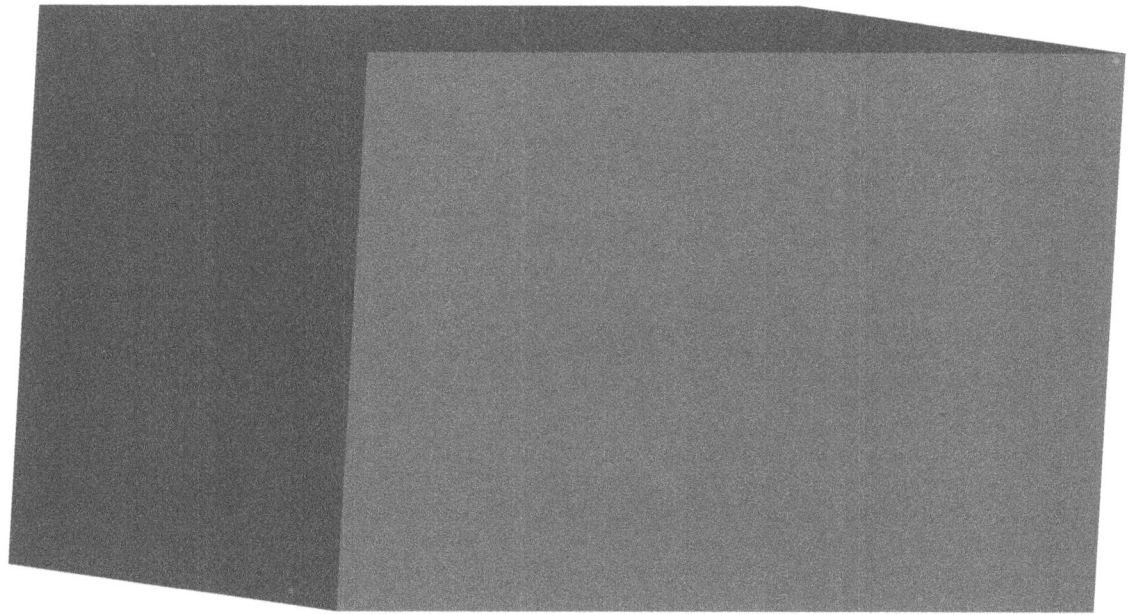

Sextangular
Schism

Where?

Oh, there?

Cool.

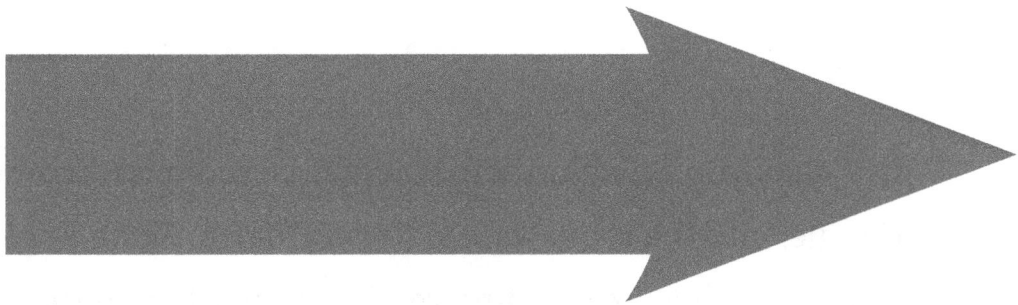

Arrow

Just when you thought there couldn't be room for another triangle, into the room walked Roger Duarte, Acute Angled Scalene Triangle extraordinaire. He points where he wants, he follows no rules, and he heeds no warnings. Cause he's long, and he's strong, and he's about to get... us into an intellectual property dispute.

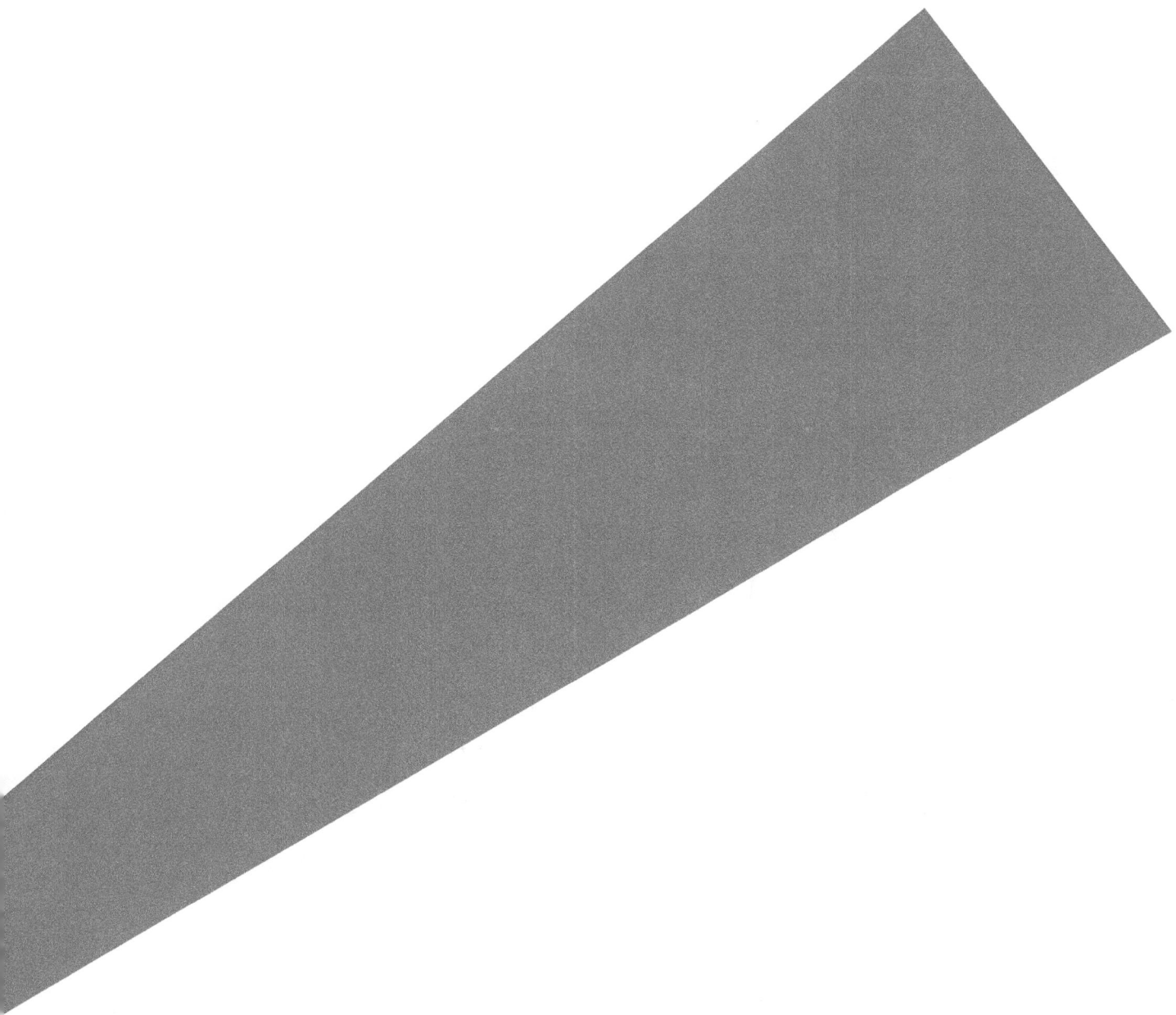

Roger Duarte

Curvilinear Triangles. Without them, we wouldn't have the guitar pick, or the... Curvilinear Triangle.

No, seriously, the Curvilinear Triangle is everything the normal triangle is except without the load-bearing capacity. It doesn't matter, Lucy-Marie ain't for using. this girl's for lovin' on. Just look at those luscious curves.

Lucy-Marie
Porthos

Not just for the military-industrial complex anymore.

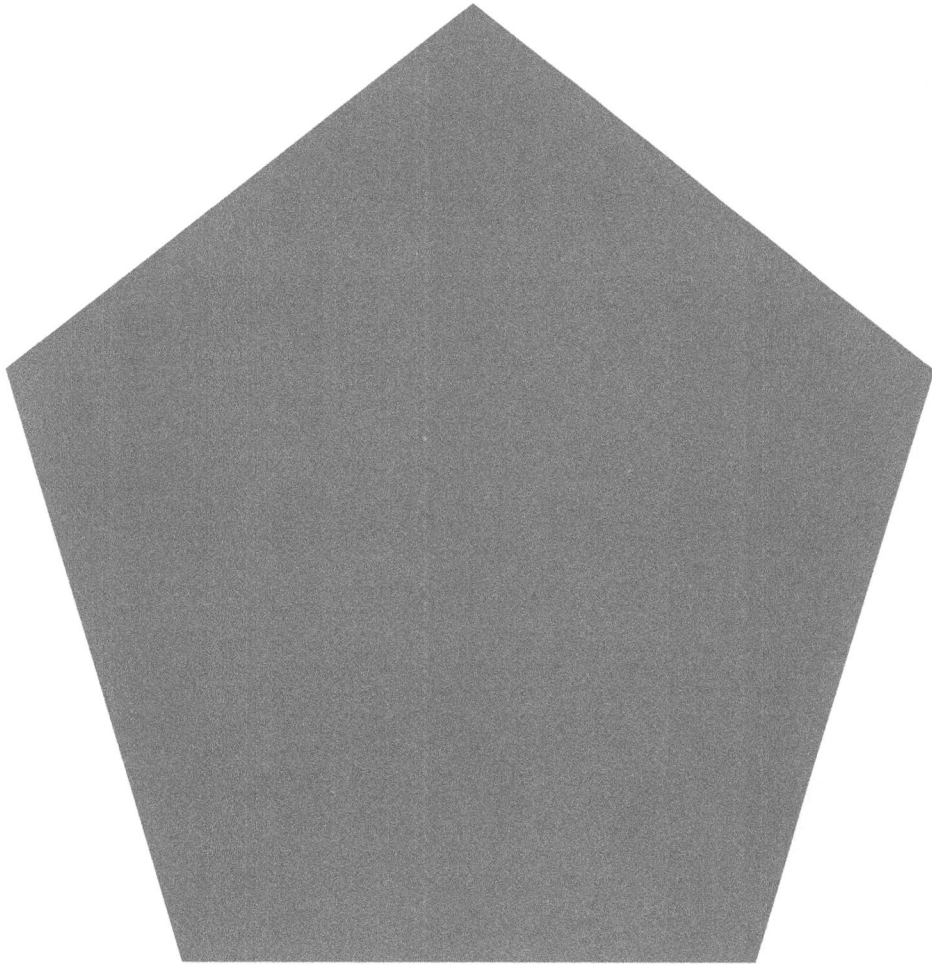

General Mayhem (ret.)

Some Octohedrons are just Octohedrons. Some are Octohedons, and those are the ones you want to look out for, either because you want a night of hot, hot, sweaty action with lots of rough edges and points, or because you don't. This shape is a live wire, so watch yourself.

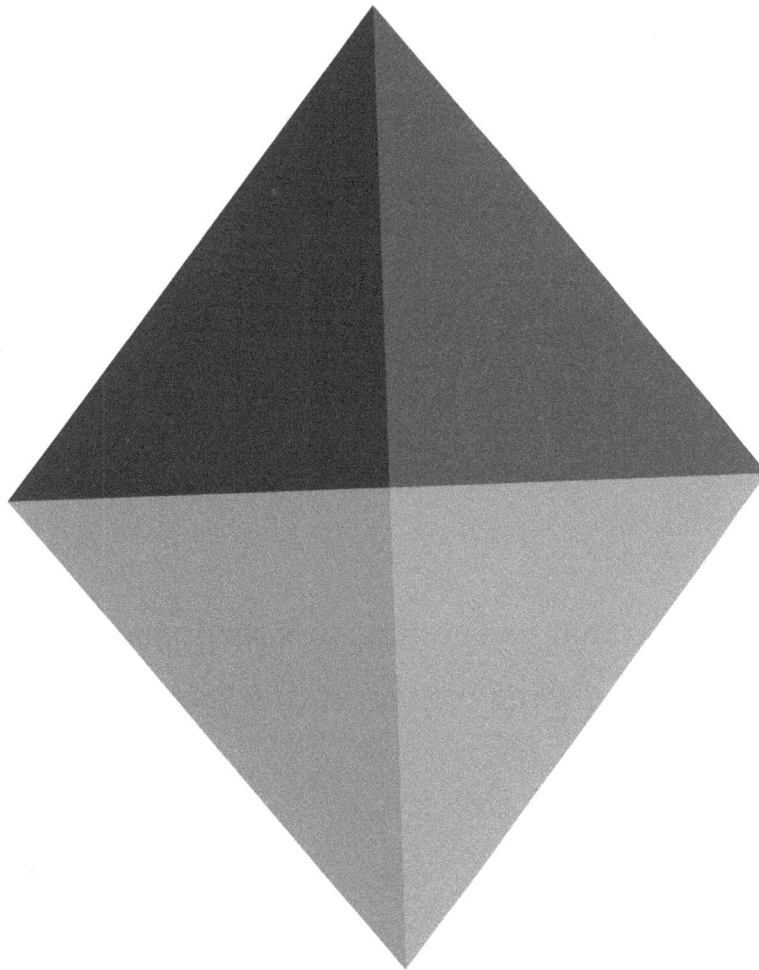

Octohedonism

Should've seen that one coming. It's really just turned into a pissing contest at this point.

Pentalong

The Icosahedron can be a bit unnecessarily confrontational, and certainly more than a touch braggy. Take, for your example, this specimen, who's managed to both elevate himself to epic proportions and insult anyone who might inquire with his name choice.

Way to be a dick. We get it, you've got a lot of sides.

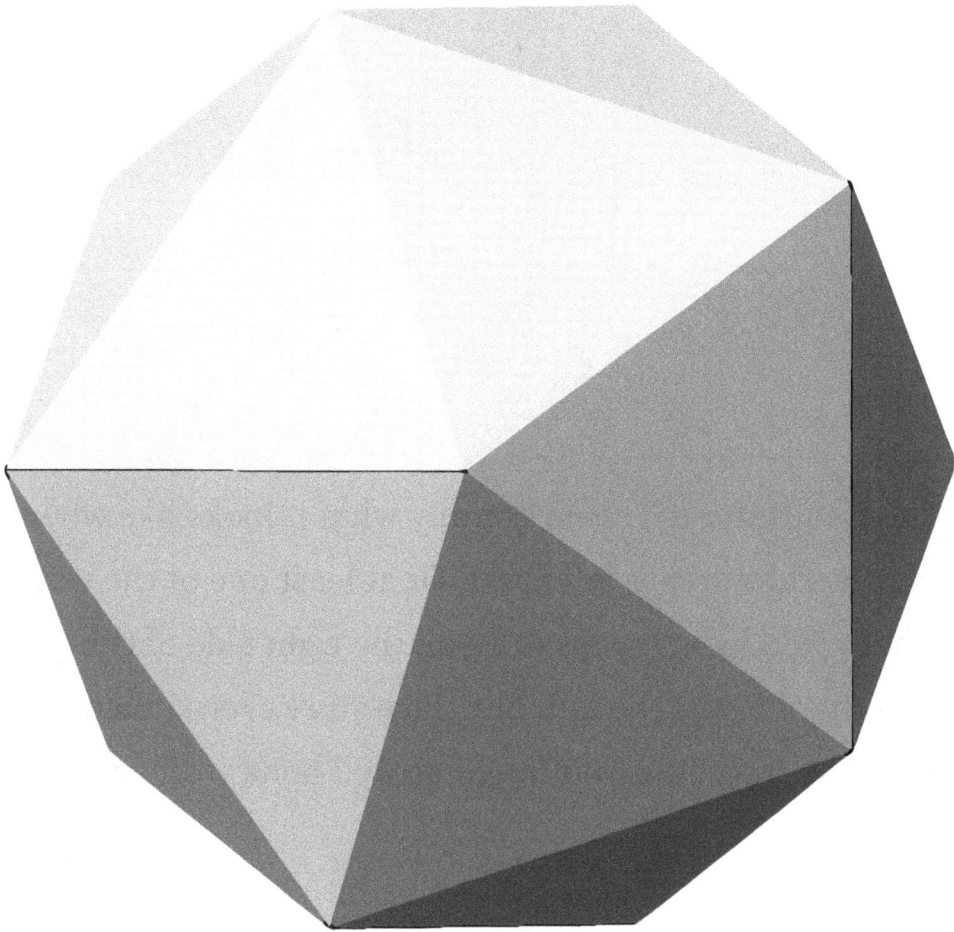

Starship
Your Mom

The Hemisphere. This is literally what it looks like when your world starts to fall apart. Or at least one of the ways that *could* look. It pays to be on the right side of things when the shit hits the fan. But since you never know which side is the right side, you might as well bone while you can.

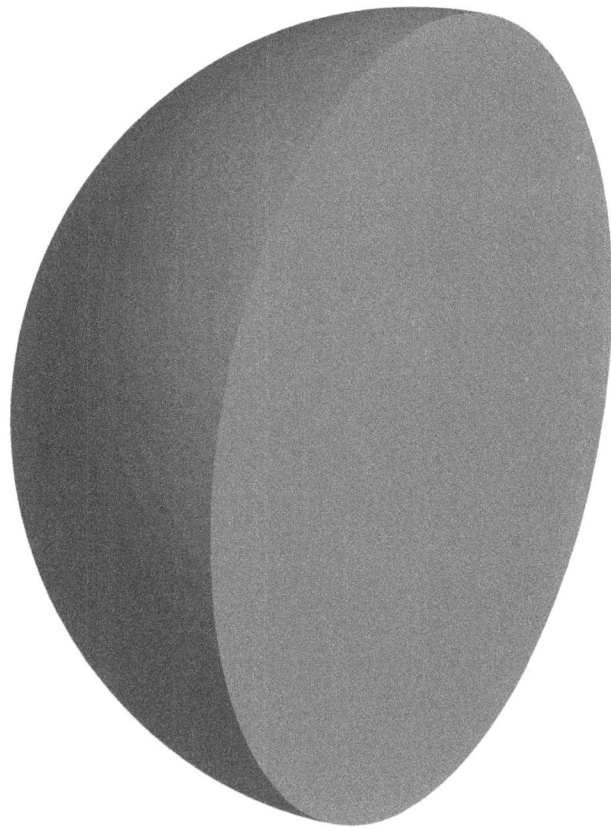

The End

www.ingramcontent.com/pod-product-compliance
Lightning Source LLC
Chambersburg PA
CBHW081945070426
42450CB00016BA/3426